JOHN THOMPSON'S
EASIEST PIANO COURSE
FIRST HALLOWEEN HITS
Arranged by Christopher Hussey

Funeral March Frédéric Chopin 2

Spooky Scary Skeletons Andrew Gold 4

The Sorcerer's Apprentice Paul Dukas 6

Which Witch Is Which? Mickey Mouse and Goofy 8

Someday from *Zombies* 10

Black Magic Little Mix 12

Halloween Sharks from *Baby Shark* 14

Evil Like Me from *Descendants* 16

Ding-Dong! The Witch Is Dead from *The Wizard of Oz* 18

Jack's Lament from *The Nightmare Before Christmas* 20

The Phantom of the Opera from *The Phantom of the Opera* 22

I'm in Love with a Monster from *Hotel Transylvania 2* 24

Friends on the Other Side from *The Princess and the Frog* 26

In the Hall of the Mountain King Edvard Grieg 28

The Witch Pyotr Il'yich Tchaikovsky 30

Teachers and Parents. This collection of spooky favorites, arranged in the John Thompson tradition, is intended as supplementary material for advancing young pianists in the Easiest Piano Course or other similar methods. Listed in the suggested order of study, most students can begin playing the first few arrangements after Part 1, and the difficulty level in this collection progresses through to Parts 3 and 4. The pieces may also be used for sight-reading practice by more advanced students.

ISBN 978-1-70517-578-1

WILLIS MUSIC

EXCLUSIVELY DISTRIBUTED BY

HAL•LEONARD®

Visit Hal Leonard Online at
www.halleonard.com

World headquarters, contact:
Hal Leonard
7777 West Bluemound Road
Milwaukee, WI 53213
Email: info@halleonard.com

In Europe, contact:
Hal Leonard Europe Limited
1 Red Place
London, W1K 6PL
Email: info@halleonardeurope.com

In Australia, contact:
Hal Leonard Australia Pty. Ltd.
4 Lentara Court
Cheltenham, Victoria, 3192 Australia
Email: info@halleonard.com.au

Funeral March
(Marche Funèbre)
from PIANO SONATA NO. 2 IN B-FLAT MINOR, Op. 35, 3rd Mvmt.

Frédéric Chopin
Arranged by Christopher Hussey

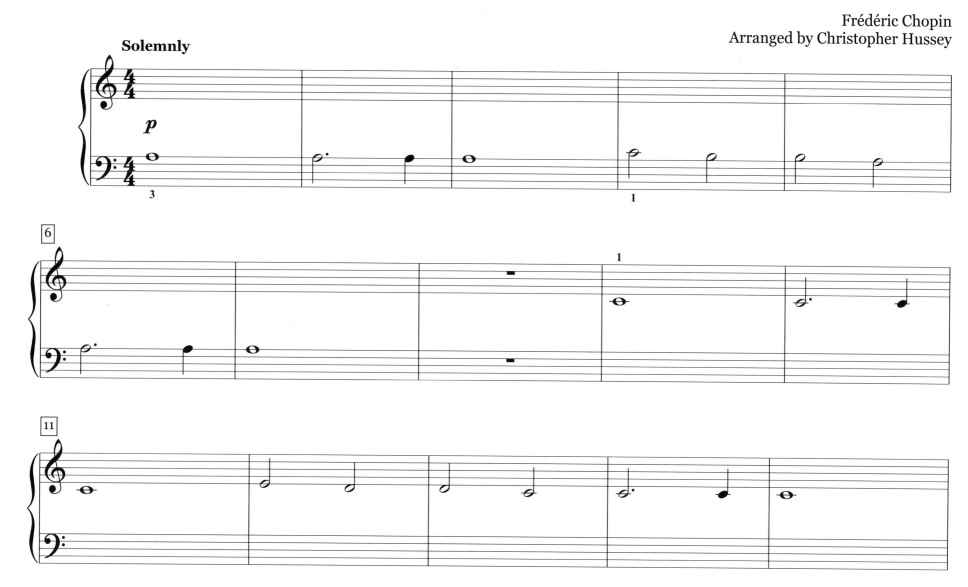

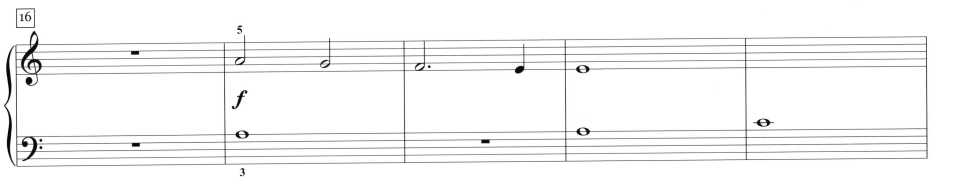

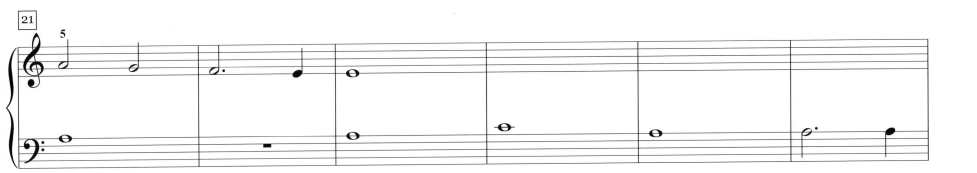

Spooky Scary Skeletons

Words and Music by
Andrew Gold
Arranged by Christopher Hussey

The Sorcerer's Apprentice

Paul Dukas
Arranged by Christopher Hussey

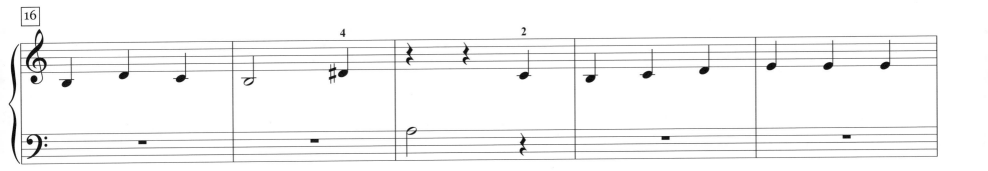

Which Witch Is Which?

from SCARY SONGS

Words and Music by Philip Baron
and Richard Friedman
Arranged by Christopher Hussey

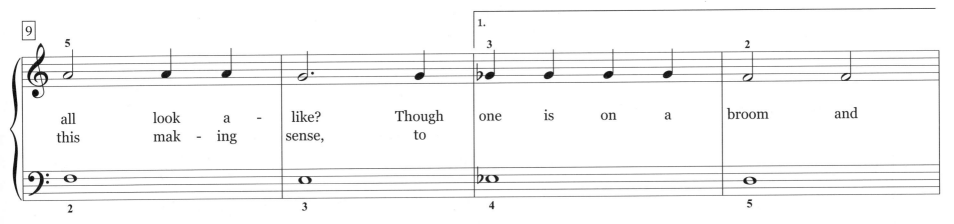

all look a - like? Though one is on a broom and
this mak - ing sense, to

one is on a bike. _____ say that they're i -

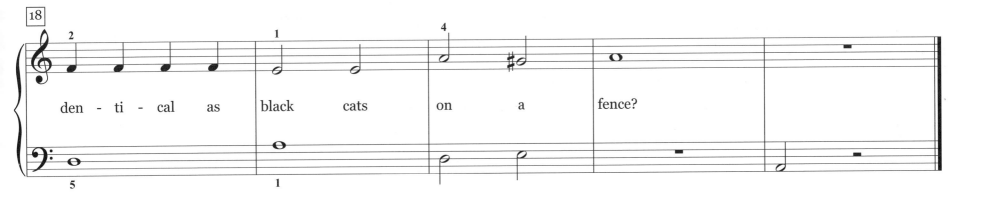

den - ti - cal as black cats on a fence?

Someday
from ZOMBIES

Music and Lyrics by Dustin Burnett
and Paula Winger
Arranged by Christopher Hussey

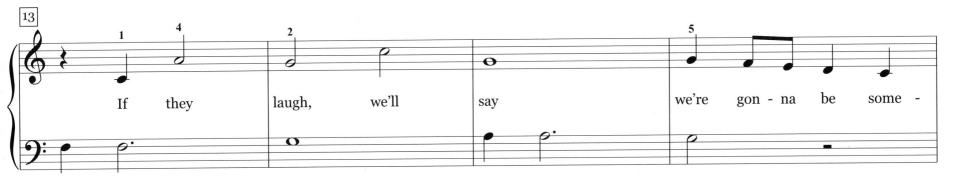

If they laugh, we'll say we're gon - na be some -

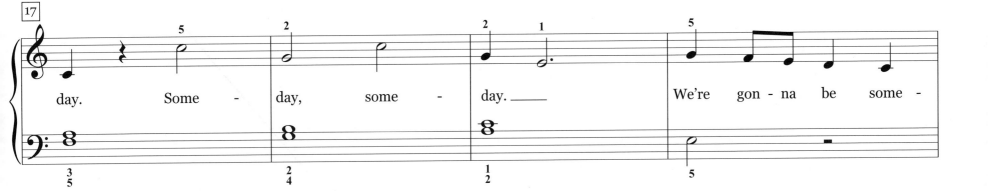

day. Some - day, some - day. ___ We're gon - na be some -

day. Some - day, some - day. ___ We're gon - na be some - day.

rit.

Black Magic

Words and Music by Camille Purcell,
Ed Drewett, Edvard Erfjord
and Henrik Michelsen
Arranged by Christopher Hussey

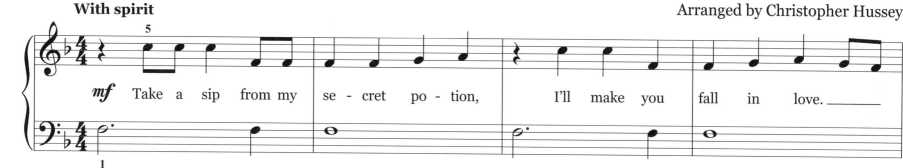

Halloween Sharks

from the TV Series BABY SHARK

Written by
Min Seok Kim
Arranged by Christopher Hussey

doo, doo, ba - by shark. *Boo!* Hal - low - een, doo, doo, doo, doo,

doo, doo, Hal - low - een, doo, doo, doo, doo, doo, doo, Hal - low -

een, doo, doo, doo, doo, doo, doo, Hal - low - een!

Evil Like Me
from DESCENDANTS

Words and Music by
Andrew Lippa
Arranged by Christopher Hussey

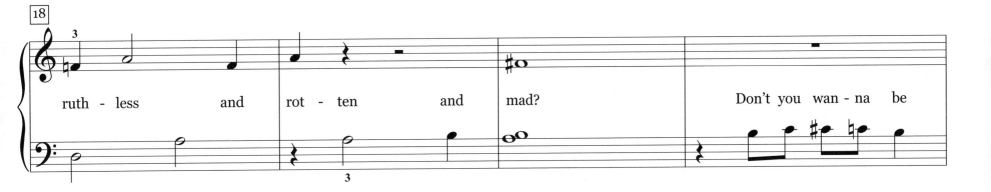

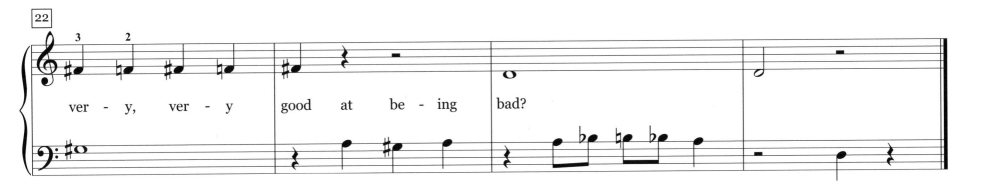

Ding-Dong! The Witch Is Dead

from THE WIZARD OF OZ

Lyric by E.Y. "Yip" Harburg
Music by Harold Arlen
Arranged by Christopher Hussey

19

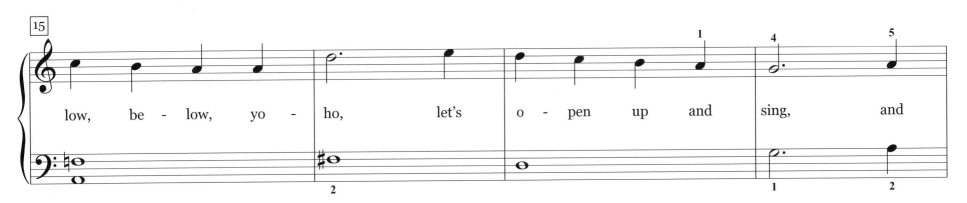

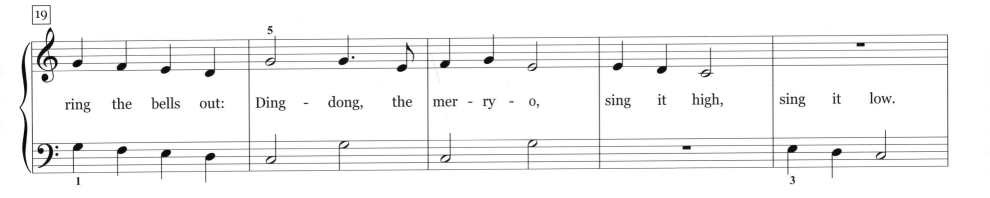

Jack's Lament
from THE NIGHTMARE BEFORE CHRISTMAS

Music and Lyrics by
Danny Elfman
Arranged by Christopher Hussey

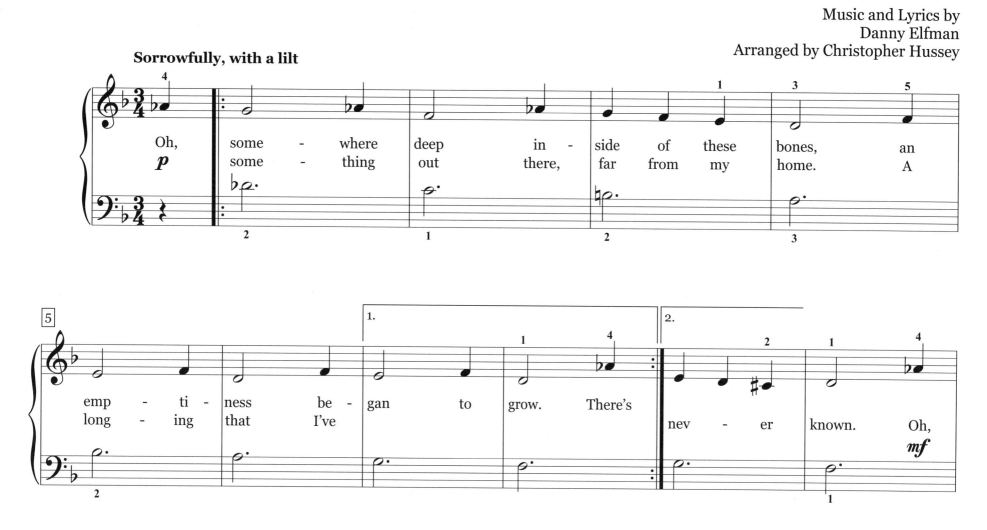

there's an emp - ty place in my bones that calls out

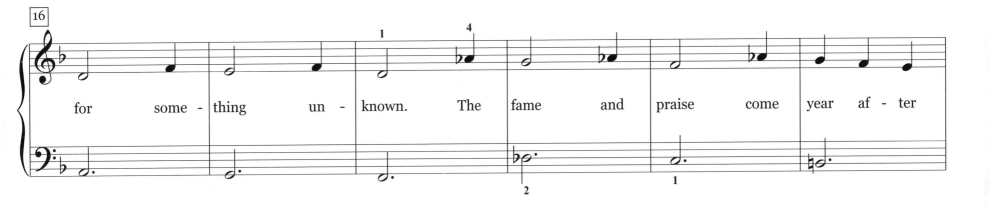

for some - thing un - known. The fame and praise come year af - ter

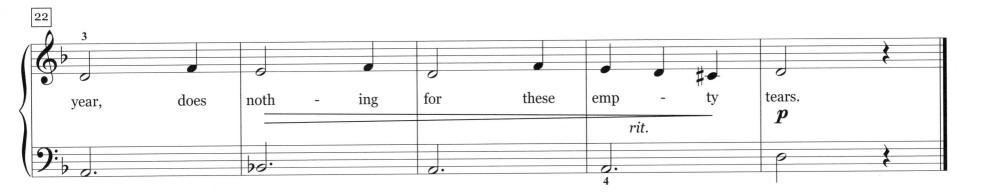

year, does noth - ing for these emp - ty tears.

rit.   ***p***

The Phantom of the Opera

from THE PHANTOM OF THE OPERA

Music by Andrew Lloyd Webber
Lyrics by Charles Hart
Additional Lyrics by Richard Stilgoe and Mike Batt

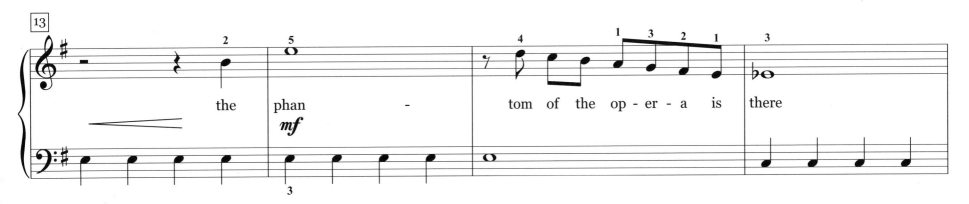

the phan - tom of the op - er - a is there

in - side my mind.

rit.

I'm in Love with a Monster
from the film HOTEL TRANSYLVANIA 2

Words and Music by Harmony Samuels,
Carmen Reece, Sara Mancuso,
Edgar Etienne and Ericka Coulter
Arranged by Christopher Hussey

Friends on the Other Side

from THE PRINCESS AND THE FROG

Music and Lyrics by
Randy Newman
Arranged by Christopher Hussey

In the Hall of the Mountain King

from PEER GYNT

Edvard Grieg
Arranged by Christopher Hussey

The Witch

from ALBUM FOR THE YOUNG, Op. 39, No. 20

Pyotr Il'yich Tchaikovsky
Arranged by Christopher Hussey

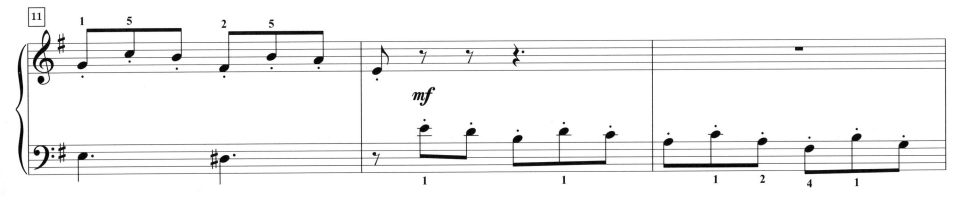

EASIEST PIANO COURSE
Supplementary Songbooks

Fun repertoire books are available as an integral part of **John Thompson's Easiest Piano Course**. Graded to work alongside the course, these pieces are ideal for pupils reaching the end of Part 2. They are invaluable for securing basic technique as well as developing musicality and enjoyment.

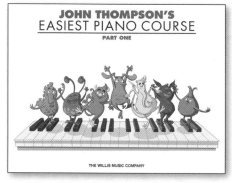

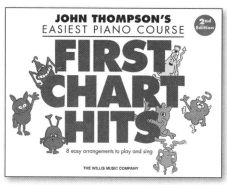

John Thompson's Easiest Piano Course

00414014 Part 1 – Book only $7.99
00414018 Part 2 – Book only $7.99
00414019 Part 3 – Book only $8.99
00414112 Part 4 – Book only $8.99

First Beethoven *arr. Hussey*
00171709 .... $8.99

First Chart Hits – 2nd Edition
00289560 .... $9.99

First Disney Songs *arr. Miller*
00416880 .... $10.99

Also available:

First Children's Songs *arr. Hussey*
00282895 .... $9.99

First Classics
00406347 .... $8.99

First Disney Favorites *arr. Hussey*
00319587 .... $10.99

First Mozart *arr. Hussey*
00171851 .... $9.99

First Nursery Rhymes
00406229 .... $8.99

First Worship Songs *arr. Austin*
00416892 .... $10.99

First Jazz Tunes *arr. Baumgartner*
00120872 .... $8.99

First Pop Songs *arr. Miller*
00416954 .... $10.99

First Showtunes *arr. Hussey*
00282907 .... $9.99

WILLIS MUSIC

EXCLUSIVELY DISTRIBUTED BY
HAL•LEONARD®

Prices, contents and availability subject to change without notice.   Disney Characters and Artwork TM & © 2019 Disney   View complete songlists and more songbooks on **www.halleonard.com**